WASTE

WASTE

EMILY TODER

BLAZEVOX[BOOKS]
Buffalo, New York

Printed in the United States of America

Interior design and typesetting by Geoffrey Gatza
Cover Art: Lower half of a human head in the round;
Collection of The Metropolitan Museum of Art. 9th century
B.C., Hasanlu, Iran.

First Edition
ISBN: 978-1-60964-327-0
Library of Congress Control Number: 2018951452

BlazeVOX [books]
131 Euclid Ave
Kenmore, NY 14217
Editor@blazevox.org

publisher of weird little books

BlazeVOX [books]

blazevox.org

21 20 19 18 17 16 15 14 13 12 01 02 03 04 05 06 07 08 09 10

BlazeVOX

Acknowledgments

Thank you to the editors of *Tenderloin, Forklift, Ohio, Interrupture, Pouch*, and *The Learned Pig*, in which some of these poems first appeared.

Thank you to Francesca Chabrier, Roger Craik, Cassandra Gillig, Anjali Khosla, and Amy Lawless.

for Mike Pfaff

WASTE

The whole world consists of pointless wastes of strength.

—Thomas Bernhard

■

Waste's sad
Waste's sad form is sad
not cause it's dead
but because it's still alive
Attracting live bugs
appealing to live vermin
wafting in the air of crafty birds
booty to living raccoons
As though in need of attention,
wailing, waste's a stinking
forfeiture of
"power"

■

I moved to the city
from the country
because of people;
because of cows
Some time ago
Lydia Davis moved from the city
to the country
but the cows distracted her
she said she moved there for peace and quiet
but the cows out her kitchen window
commanded all her attention
all day every day

She said she thought, "How
am I supposed to get any work done?"

This is not like what happened to me
but when I think of what happened to me
I like to think of this

■

Waste is fine clothing
tailored to suit disease
handed down from sick,
fun forebears
by fit descendants
who hardly dance

■

To waste food is bad
and thoughtless but it's nothing
next to wasting a life,
the meaning of which
people are generally hesitant
to define, if not unwilling
to mention altogether because it's
frightening, maybe
more frightening than death?
I bet for some people
it is

■

Waste's sad
Waste's swollen formless
hollowness is sad
Waste's sad
Waste's where life meets death
but does not go to it

■

One dietician said wasting food
in garbage bins is actually better
than wasting that same food in your body
that food which you are too guilty to toss

But it is really hard to know
what toll a caloric excess
actually takes on the organs

And as it disintegrates by the enzymes
who can know what power it brings

And who can say what power it has
doing this invisibly
out of sight and politically rewardingly

And who can say that it rots at all
inside the gleaming coils

Yes, it's technically the charge of the dietician
to know how it affects these tracts
But really, who can know?

■

There's a lot of stuff that's called waste
circumstantially or idiomatically but actually
it isn't:

Shit isn't waste
until it doesn't go
in the earth

Toxic waste's only waste cause anything
toxic's waste

Waste is not revocable
and not finalized
it's infinite

People handmaking artifacts
arduously for people can be a form of waste
not because the artifact is destroyed
but because it fades in the sunlight
while the people break or at least
don't speak
In that situation the people are not technically
wasted but the torque of their efforts is
dead

Time wasted is a misnomer for whatever
one is afraid to experience

instead of kissing his sleeve

Money wasted is the confusion of extravagance
with satisfaction
I mean the conflation of tangible trade
with experience
I mean wasting money's a great privilege
the squanderers on some level must revel in

A wasted opportunity is a fruit of shyness
or of foresight but usually of doubt
or shyness; self-doubt
And it appears later boldly,
an exercise in bogus retrospect

Basically what I'm saying is
it doesn't exist
Basically I'm saying these stock phrases
which are always metaphors are distracting
and take away from the real meaning
of "waste" or "wasted"

The thing about an entire life wasted
is it's difficult to talk about it
Try going out and talking about it,
it's incredibly tough

■

FML is not really a new or fun way of saying
"I have wasted my life"
It's more like saying "I can't stand a snag
in this perfunctory glory I'm living"
It's basically saying "This doesn't suit my life
which is clearly not being wasted"
People who say FML are proud
and never IRL pronounce it

■

I think a mother can see waste in her child
not only by looking at the child
but by listening to what she or he says
The mother can crystallize this for herself painfully
by remembering a similar moment
in the life of the child,
a moment in the child's childhood
that foreshadowed the waste
that she knew would eventually ensue
The mother might then take some blame
upon herself, but she mustn't;
she must go to her other child
and realize this shit is out of her control

■

Silence is seldom a waste but it's not impossible

Throwing a toy down a garbage chute is always
a traumatic waste

A waste is typically an irreversible abuse of the hope
people can have in people or whatever
brings comfort

Ephemerality has nothing to do with waste

Waste is the rejection of the mediocre promise
feeding avidly the waking heart or eye

Waste is to weep for the undead

■

Is it a waste to study something
you are never tested on?
No, you freaking lowlife

Is it a waste to set aflame
a house full of paintings?
No.

■

I liked my boyfriend
who believed it was impossible to waste time
I agreed with him so we never spoke of it
but now I think it wouldn't have been so bad
to get his thoughts on the matter
It probably would've been useful
All these years later I wonder
why did he think it was so impossible?
Can he still think this?
How can he?
I don't think it's a waste to wonder
I find it useful
and eventually I conclude he now thinks
it actually *is* possible to waste time
and a whole host of other things
As I twist my braids
I deduce he ages
most sure of this

■

Some day I want to tell someone
"Don't waste your breath,"
knowing that whatever words
they're about to utter are gonna be
so illegitimate,
they might as well not breathe
the air to sound them
Then I will have saved that person that breath
that otherwise would have been wasted

■

If the Cold War had been about
putting garbage on other planets
it could've been called
the Waste Race
Luckily it was just about military dominance
disguised as ways of life
Anyway this period was maybe the least wasteful
of its kind

■

In England this poem would have to be different
so as to in some way account for the use
of the term "rubbish"

Otherwise it would be largely the same
except that in that land I would not write it

I would find the thin palm
in Cornwall he surfs by

In England I could touch the ancient ceiling

I would plant my elbows in some heath
or moor

His face would squint from the winds
off some cliffs or crags

I think David Sedaris picked up the rubbish
in England & learned a lot from it

■

Once, after a beer,
my friend said he'd take the train
to where he was staying
so as not to "waste"
his 3-day unlimited MetroCard
he'd bought the other day

I told him that what's done is done
and that there was nothing
he could do to not waste that card
from here on out,
short of taking a cab, or buying
the illusion of more limitlessness
for a finite period of days

Did I just want him to walk me home
through my unsafe neighborhood?
Or did I want him to feel free
from the MTA?

I don't know

I believed in what I said

■

I think "wastecase"
could be a good term
for a basketcase whose life
is wasted
That or a dumpster
a lunatic is living in
That or a person who
cannot make a bit of progress
and makes calls in the night
That or in the dawn

■

It's funny that "wasted"
colloquially can mean "drunk" or "high"
It's funny cause being those things
can lead some people
straight to ruin
Still, "drunk" and "high" and "wasted"
are not synonyms
in my book

■

Literal waste is less sad than figurative waste
Tangible waste is smelly but easier to take
Waste relying on imagery is worse than actual waste
Waste that is subjective is difficult to prove but we do
Physical waste can stink but the stinkiest of it
      degrades
Odorless waste can last indefinitely
Concepts of waste last forever and are rank
Waste that is imagined is powered by electrical
      charges
I would rather live in a trash heap
than harbor such a sensation
Visible waste is transported strategically to unseen
      sites
The mass of real waste weighs a lot without density
Visibly discernible waste is more tolerable than
      symbolic waste
Abstract waste can rattle the mind and degrade the
      body
Allegorical waste is hard to let go of
I would rather settle down to sleep in real debris

■

Is it a waste or is it not a waste
to engage in trauma the brain blacks out after anyway

Well it's not a waste, because without engaging
you would not have made it out of there

Well, but of course it is a waste

■

I was born in New York
but I am not very tough
I was born in New York City but I
have a jelly for a skin, but my heart
is more like a frozen jelly

When I picture it I picture a slab
with salt all over it getting flung
on a fleur de lis, does that work?

New York is great for being free and lost
and with great loss and freedom you can
interact a whole lot, you can interact constantly
with souls you can't gauge

In New York you can do this all day long
and not achieve so much

The expenditure of such energy
isn't wasteful tho cause it helps you
prepare for the real thing,
and you can fill your life up
with anecdotes

You can spend your life telling strangers
anecdotes about other strangers
feeling close to them all, giving high fives

You can get an illusion of pleasing them
by holding their doors
and I like to lift strollers up also out of the subway

■

It's a waste for the police to ask
for your help
or for mine

We're doing all we can
to stay out of their way

We want to look after
one another in a private way

■

Is a muddled cucumber
a waste
of the cucumber?

Not with
Cazadores Blanco
chili agave & lime

Not with 2 oz. ice
4 oz. vodka & mint

Not with 1½ oz. Hendrick's
¼ oz. St. Germain
& a twist of lemon

Not with a twinge from the wits
Not with a twitch of the gut
Not in a gimlet
Not in a lobby
Not in the past

■

That boyfriend I mentioned who thought
you couldn't waste time
wasted a marriage

but not the rest of his life

but some of my spirit

but not any money

but his entire time

but his wife and girlfriend's ribs

but not his life

but what stood in for stamina

but not his life

but my soft wetness

but not his enjoyment of life

but my mind

■

Leaves twisting in a basement
Parched soil lodging the leaves
Unknowable nitrogen everywhere
Water rushing flatly above the pot in pipes
And all the still water lying just out of reach
Bugs that drown in the faraway water
Sunlight on the cables

■

Pete McEntegart felt like he wasted six months
of his life serving on the trial of Dennis Kozlowski
when it was declared a mistrial, due to 1 sketchy juror

Pete was ready to convict and felt frustrated
with this lame peer, who whimsically doubted in the
the defendant's careful collusion or evil

Throughout the fourteen days of deliberation,
Pete was anxious to see justice served
and I think he wanted to see that CEO locked up
for the theft he'd committed, and punished
for the broken dreams that the theft broke

But mostly, he wanted to think that all that time
he'd spent had not been a waste:
the time in the hotel, far away from his wife & family
the times in the hotel never talking to anybody
the time with his face in the lamp....

Sure, he wanted to participate in the justice system,
which he felt was counting on him & his eleven peers
but mostly he ached to know that his efforts had been
valuable, and he longed to hear a sentence spoken

When the next jury easily rendered a verdict
was he slightly jealous?
Yeah and it contributed substantially
to his feeling that the six months had been a waste

■

What's the opposite of waste?
Perhaps it is a reasonable garden plot
It could be a modest patch of sprout
The arduous voyage of aliens...
Soaps or crayons that regenerate
It could be a last glimpse at the eyeball
of your love as it neglects to study you
A comet perfectly positioned...
An asteroid positioned perfectly
A lot of examples could come in second chances
never given
In not a rebirth, but a whole nother birth
The real opposite of waste calls for paranormal
interventions and thus some paranormal beliefs
The true opposite of waste relies lamely
on the unfeasible application of hindsight
The opposite of waste without bending the rules
of time is limited to isolated examples
of shocking practicality that occur in despair
The opposite of waste is worms in the waste
The opposite of waste is fruitful old waste
Some might say it's a miracle baby
but that wouldn't cut it for me

■

Waste is the body dying
before birthing

I'm as prejudiced
as the universe is
in this pronouncement

Waste is tubes narrowed
preventatively
That's just not for me

Nor is cryogenics, which is actually
a perfect word

Nothing centrifugal should
be part of my life in any way

I'm on a plane and my carry-on fell gently
onto a woman
I'm on my way back, since I accomplished
what I had wanted to have accomplished

Now I am accomplished
Now I'm in airplane mode

Waste could be leaving something good to no one

■

Wasting life
is the easiest thing to do in the world
in the moment
in which you're doing it
and later, in the ensuing moments
which are then hollowed out,
dry or dried from the futility you did previously
descending stairs or even soft hills

■

Wasting life
is the easiest thing
to do in the world,
I can do it in my sleep

I do it whilst I creatively
dream alternatives for
me and you, yes
I do it while I am resting my head
I can do it on my commute
effortlessly I can while I am repotting a plant

Wasting life is so easy
I don't even have to be awake to do it,
I can do it asleep on planes or ferries
I can do it beside men whom I love
to the ends of the earth

Sometimes I make small talk
while I'm doing it,
just to pass the time

■

When movie actors
pour tall bottles of alcohol
down sink drains in movies
about alcoholism
they're not really wasting alcohol
because it's fake alcohol
and their characters aren't really wasting it
cause they're determined to get better
This is usually about 20 minutes into the movie,
when we're still getting to know the character

■

Years upon years of study
at accredited universities
can be wasted by a mind
that is in the gutter
It can be wasted by a mind
that is easily washed, and swayed
It's wasted by a mind
which reads voraciously but too late
A mind already formed,
formed and shaped before all that reading
A mind that admires language
and speaks articulately
with other language lovers
never knowing the lovers

■

It's a waste
nothing comes of
the sexual tension
of Law & Order SVU

This pair of investigators never touches
They make sweet criminals crack
all without touching
He has four kids
She has none, cause her dates
are really intimidated
They speak with their eyes
Surprisingly she chops her hair
He cries once a season

Together they go to different addresses
barely brushing
In the last ten minutes the guilty guest star
tells them: "You don't understand"
But they do, they do

The whole hour they've understood
but they will never touch
and amid the clarinets backdrop
and amid the beautiful bridge brimming with vice,
one realizes it would never work

He has to go home every night
to the wife the show shows sometimes
(as well as the eldest daughter,
who is sexually active, making him quake)
and he must be a loyal stony husband to her
while Olivia sits alone, writhing, acting
as the sole legal guardian for twenty
unwed mothers' underweight NICU babies
she decides to keep alive, ignoring
the prognoses of hot doctors
with whom she also cannot get involved

■

TVs've helped me waste my life
I know I couldn't have done it alone
I needed negative aspiration
to realize who I was
and at one other point who I was
and to compare those

Baby boomers told me not to worry
and tender contemporaries in hot palms
in the sunsets I saw faded into a nonsense for me
which I found sickening
if I was drinking
and my own grandmothers
were too sweet to ever believe me
and they each died thinking about me in a really
positive way

■

There can be no waste
without an exhausting
endurance

The inexhaustiveness
of ongoing exhaustion
is the prelude to waste

Waste comes out
of unbounded exertion
ever-lasting

When waste begins
it can look like anything
No one has ever seen waste end

■

My friend said in an email:
"Waste is an independent variable"

I didn't know what to make of it
I guess waste operates without help?

He is writing a book
called *Let x Equal* which I think
will be brilliant and long
It's a textbook

My friend had a fender bender
that wasn't a big deal
He said he had a great hope in me
He lives in a high altitude

He knows the object of my life
He drives my same car

My friend verified all my ideas
and then defied them sort of identically
which I enjoy hugely

My friend and I talk on our landlines
so I can really hear him

He sings in the shower
He has wasted his talent, he says

He is remarkable at physics
and is also a musical genius
This friend knows everything

My friend speaks from the vantage of outcomes
on mountains

I'm lost cause there's no stars
in the city

My friend is great at piano
My friend is very mature

But he has never unpacked his amps
My friend is very mature but
all his music is in its cases

Golf balls land on his balcony

This friend soothes me a lot simply
by being older and more professional

And he actually lives in the present
My friend tackles each moment he's in

I don't use him as a messenger
I used to but I don't anymore

Now I let him be in the moment

■

The nature of some boys was disturbed
when they were taught to think of masturbation
as waste

This threw off their nature
in a way I don't know

I don't know what it was like
as they continued to grow
or how their desire felt
like guilt coming into nothing,
or even into a woman, for that matter,
into a barrier in the woman,
or in a man, for that matter,
but I don't think they should feel guilty,
those men and boys
I think they should feel relieved

■

You think in the animal kingdom
there's no waste
since you know better
than to lend dull human qualities
unto speechless black eyes
but actually there's a lot

If you don't believe me,
get out of the city
look in the dirt
dig a little bit with your claws
stand in what you have dug
and empty your pockets

■

Well-written WikiHow articles on time travel

■

Tribalism scandalizing
otherwise unremarkable
love, messing people's
lives up in that
important way

■

Banana trees fruit only once
but it's not a waste cause the decay actually
lays the ground
for the next banana

■

Not the weddings;
the centerpieces

Not the centerpieces;
the centerpieces sulking

Not the sulking;
the crumbling
of the foamy center
of the centerpiece

Sure, the crumbling,
but moreover,
the disintegration

The disintegrated sea-green
foam riding home to cheer
the luridly stripped homes
of the positive-thinking

The broken sea-glass-green
centerpiece's center, scattering
itself about in luxury
taxi backseats
modeling at last the grace of
the structure it fakes

■

Even forgotten parties
are not wastes

Any party your soul came to
was not a waste

Even expensive parties
you threw in debt

Even parties you made
mistakes at are worthwhile

Any party you were able
to sway at with some love

I am thinking of one party
in particular but really

This applies to all the long
forgotten parties

This one goes out to all the sequins
and all the balloons out there

This one is for the untouched
cakes and ideas

■

I don't think a failed campaign
is necessarily a waste
because in it and through it
some ideas can change and some
changes to ideas can be good

I know that certain failed campaigns
have raised an awareness
of issues among people who
weren't very aware of
those issues previously

I know that a campaign
changed somebody's
loved one's ideas, probably

The energy of the one campaigning
was not wasted either because
after all, it was a form of exercise
and his or her body could benefit from that
though surely there were health
drawbacks to the schedule

The money spent on the campaign
obviously is lost for nothing,
save the abovementioned ideas changing
in the hearts of the right ones' loved ones

The efforts of the volunteers
have positive reverberations
and build a forgotten confidence

The total cost of a campaign
is so enormous

■

It's sort of a waste to be romanced by a diplomat
who's only in town for the U.N.
It's wasteful of resources, which diplomats
are supposed to know are limited!
It's wasteful of that resource that has no end
and diplomats can't understand that
It's wasteful because you can learn to waltz
only to fall down upon a new culture
It's a waste to fall down around international cuisine
It's a waste to not taste his and his people's food

It's a waste to botch a waltz
It's a waste to watch the proceedings on YouTube
It's a shame the diplomat moves fast
around the world without you
The worst thing of all is not knowing how to speak
the five languages
The worst thing of all is not knowing one language
Dreaming's also the worst thing of all

■

I get it, if you can make it here,
you'll make it anywhere

But if you can't make it here,
can you make it anywhere else?
or just someplace else?

Where can you make it?

I would like to listen to a song about that

■

Meerkats are among the most wasteful animals
In the Kalahari, they waste not the scarce resources
all about them, but their own offspring
all around them, and thus their selves

They live in matriarchies
ruled by petty mothers
who regularly avenge their birthing daughters,
shutting them out

The shunning of the fertile
is biologically wasteful, but also mean
– I mean the shunning of it until it is dead –
and like all other disowning, emotionally
devastating

You can see the hurt in the still and stiff
pose of the excommunicated female
who knows she'll die of clanlessness,
her black eyes darting dark and sharp in the heat
her cowered "praying" arms limp and matte
her fur by her ears scruffy and clumped
from the stress and from the pain
and it is all she can do to pivot
while her blind and pink young only feet below her
are blind and pink

Her mother discovers them and brings them up
just after she's roasted in the sun
then her mother has further daughters
and those daughters further daughters
For how long can this go on
Forever

■

Animals don't do anything wrong
Animals are perfect

Animals are perfectly natural
Wild animals are perfect

Animals are perfect naturally
Natural animals are wild

Wild animals are natural
Naturally animals are perfect

Animals are wildly natural
Perfect animals are wild

Natural animals are perfect
The perfect animal is vulnerable

It is perfectly normal
for the vulnerable animal
to regret its life

■

Most animals waste animals
A good deal engage in light-hearted
shredding of their prey
Everyone knows some animal who has
played crudely with a half-dead
other animal
leaving its richness to wither blithely

The only ones who leave no leftovers
are those in the rodentia order
whose relentless teeth
must always feed, not necessarily on food
This order is arguably the most tortured
of the entire kingdom

Animals waste other animals'
valuable bodies, because they don't know how
to wield tools of their like bones
and most don't need additional fur, or skin

The animals enjoy themselves
They find shelter and go to sleep
Animals rear their young roughly
and when it looks cute to us,
cutely, and virally,
and it's very restorative

The cutest things I've ever seen,
I realize, I've never seen
I don't want to put a loris on a piano

I think animals are cute
in an ancient way

■

The new moon
can seem like a waste
of the enormous
energy of the sun
but this is just one
of Earth's great illusions

If you're not on Earth
this kind of moon is not
a thing

The moon's silvery
blindingness is steady

The sun's power
will not be wasted

■

I waste years upon years of my youth
and of my maturity
and of my parents' relative youth
and of the literal youth of the children
in my life and of the "youthful spirit"
at work in the seniors in my life, who are
the ones who advise most against
wasting your life cause they understand truly
the body's importance
Hardly moving their bodies
they envy me hardly

So now and again I reach out to him
because once my face was behind an umbrella
and even then he grabbed for my wrist

■

It's a waste to bring a non-Jew
to an awkward Jewish ceremony
even as he is falling in love with you…
It's wasteful to attend an authentic Jewish ceremony
the very next day alone, his large computer
shifting in the dark backseat to your empty house
rid of leavened bread and things
even as you are falling in love…

Waste doesn't distinguish
between absence and presence and
waste does not discriminate

■

Garbage in natural landscapes is particularly touching
when you recognize it you feel
a special twinge

You touch it with your boot
and try to carry on but it's useless
You should pick it up

You should buy in bulk
Buy goods without packaging, that is,
if you can't trade your goods for services,
or different goods

That is, I think,
a different economy

That is an important technicality
that makes a major difference
that we overlook with a convincing convenience

One sad example is a tissue stuck on a cactus

■

The executive assistant at my new job
tapes print-outs of strangled seals
by the recycling bins in the office
and is understandably upset
when people are not so moved by them
so as to modify their behavior
accordingly and recycle

All people should be like her
and also they need to change their behavior

I wish I could laminate the print-outs
without offending her

But my number-one dream would be to be a spider
and hang off my own silk for absolutely nothing

■

I like the trope wherein ex-lovers
ask each other years later if they're happy
In the trope, they're like, "No, but I'm good"
cause their situation's safe and/or youth-oriented

Few of the characters feel they have wasted their lives
as a result of the loves but every now and then
you will find a feature that attempts to annually
quantify such a phenomenon

I haven't been close enough to this trope
to gauge its poignancy
I don't know if it's true for anybody
in real life, or for anybody's sick mind
in real life

When it happens on network TV
the writers are just doing their jobs
but when it happens in independent films
you just have to weep and leave
the theater with the other people and stuff
your face in your gloves like a grownup
rubbing your eyes economically cause enough
is enough

■

The executive assistant said her rent money
goes to waste each month cause she practically
lives at her boyfriend's now

This is the most pleasant instance of waste
I can think of and I don't want her
to read anything I write

■

Memory lane is hideous

Its cobble is broken
& you can no longer afford
the prices

If walking down memory lane
ever makes you feel old you don't think enough
about the sediment the lane is made up of

If you should ever feel old and broke
walking down memory lane
you should probably wait
to become older and more broke
& try it again

Memory lane is no joke
Memory is actually a real footpath
in the space-time no one can feel

The metaphor of the lane
is a nice try but the past
is actually happening

■

Each time I exert myself it results in another waste
but each time it's prettier and more expedient
A shoebox can be a rich abyss
Actually, it works with anything

■

For a little while I worked at the best bookstore
in New York
and with my 40% discount I bought just one book:
a *Dover* edition

This is a casual but striking waste
Not a waste of money, per se,
but a waste of its conservation, which is imaginary
and powerful

In other words, I wasted a useful illusion that was
valuable, and which moves people though it does not
exist, but which moved me through my shifts
cause throughout them, I thought of some kind of
reward, forgetting that I was at work and my salary
was the reward, only to remember that I shouldn't
live in New York, and I don't deserve a new book
anyway cause I'm never going to finish *Middlemarch*
which is nice because I can forever trust
she is going to eventually leave that sexless bozo

■

It is really the earth's time we are wasting,
not our moments of our lives
But even mourning this is assigning so great a value
to something I don't understand I cannot devote
my life to it

My thoughts on the apocalypse are complex:
I like its unknowableness so much
my first reaction is light and viscerally positive
and I can appreciate the phonetic depth
Then I am sad – the rust on school vans in vines
would make anyone sad –
but immediately I'm relieved
The infinity that endures is slightly maddening…
Thoughts of children and animals are difficult
but mostly, I am alarmingly calm when presented
with fictional images of this ultimate climax

I do not care to survive such an event
I will not kill for a can
I refuse to be alone

■

Nature trivia is an oxy-moron
There is nothing trivial about the network of rivers
at work, or about the constant swap of hydrogen
from here to there, or about the thoughtful exchange
underway amidst the roots of the forest bottoms,
delivering the richest dirt to the saplings in conduits

I would like to try to learn some of this so-called
trivia, including "trivia" about "space"
but just now I am too tired and preoccupied
with other studies, of other life forms:
Like immediately perceiving the narcissist
Like promptly detecting the narcissist at once
Like moving away speedily from this soul
And the mysterious nature of his clout
distracts me from the trees and from the seashells
It destroys the stanza
The ineffable tug of his command
corrupts the imagination of eukaryotes
and dissolves the deadness of the stars
which ironically he knows all about....
It destroys the stirring image of meiosis
and disrupts my pile of flash cards
It obliterates the beginnings of the pure glimpse
of infinity

I think that the accomplished protistologists
of the world must have had to find
very supportive partners in their lives
in order to study these unusual cells
I think that their makeup
is unattainable
And with the stability fostered within them,
they have conducted fantastic research
for all of us to read and to learn from
We who will never see the cilia

■

It's worth taking your time
to get to know someone

The value of this precaution
deepens as its fruits swell
and rot

It's great if you can walk
around the reservoir with him

■

Waste is natural and unnatural
Waste is eminently biological
but also so cultural
Waste is crudely visceral and also
crudely sociological
Waste is learned, but
not uniformly by all cultures
Each culture teaches and learns waste
in its own way
Also, within each of those cultures
there is great variation
Waste is innate, but not
inherited
All are born with and from waste
but waste is not passed down
Tolerance of waste varies
from generation to generation
Accommodation of quotidian waste
has defined the times
The times have always been defined
by these things
Histories of waste
are needed

■

I went out with a bully for four hours, when I
could have been reading *Lady Chatterley's Lover*

We talked about how the neighborhood is changing
then I lost my toothpick in my hair

If this is not the epitome of waste then take me
to the hut and make me sit on
the stump

■

Travel is a bit hard to waste but not impossible
Particularly if returning to sites already seen
I know because I did it
I thought it would help
Also, it was polite

People thought I was very young
but I was old and I did not know the future
was gonna be about the gorgeousness of the orange,
the orangeness of the yellow I saw, I didn't know
it was gonna be about a halogen overgrowth
of a pinpoint on a line of time I lived in

When I got there I made a lot of phone calls
I made calls leaning against cold walls
I wanted to feel included in humanity, and a part
of a human fabric of a kind of humankind
I went back years later to this particular site on Earth
to feel connected to that same story and to get a vibe
of my humanity's being unremarkable
After I flew home I went home and a stranger
reached out to me, which was ridiculous
because that was America by then

When I got home I summarized this to myself
but only up to this point
I was quiet and didn't move

There was a party that night and my friend crashed
my other friend's car in a tree but I wasn't there
So the next day I heard about it ten times and I
couldn't decide which of the ten stories was true
I never said anything about the waste of the travel
I just told each one of them they were right
wishing I had been there so that I could be drunk
out of my mind

■

What wasn't a waste was endangering myself
in order to feel good in my neighborhood

It was not a waste these nights I spent I never
spent on the stoop

It wasn't a waste to counter a waste with
a more fun-loving waste

The waste is not the way that when I ran
to my love I didn't stop

When even I passed a friend and I couldn't
say hi because I was in the middle of running

She didn't mind
she was happy
to see me
in such a way

That's not a waste;
It was great
to make her happy in that instant

I loved the instant I made
my mother happy

It was not a waste
when my mother managed
to look at me

It was not a waste
to run into that man's arms...

The waste is the energy the cells consume
to remind me of the running

The waste is all the food
that it takes those cells to do this

The waste is the witless neurons
sending these signals to these organs

And the way the limbs can move at will
and the beautiful feeling the body can give
and the oxygen it takes all those cells
to tell such a glorious lie

and the tireless fiery synapses that make it real
even now, when it really doesn't exist
and all the oxygen that it takes the body to do all this

■

The time to create a perfect appearance
The perfect sleep to forge deeply foolish eyes
The perfectly unwitting method of molecular renewal
The perfect chemical drug to fool the mind & organs
Perfect hair twisted into decent accessories
The charming clash of off-black all over the body
The ease of a perfect first impression and its paced
enrichment
The effortlessness of perfection in the beginning
and the efforts expended in its wake
An alleyway's perfect dimensions
The ideal location of a chemist
The optimal lozenge
The perfect mucus
The neat way flesh coats the bones
The dreamy arrangement of the internal
organs and the well-orchestrated web of veins
The careful and contained flesh that made up
the physical aspect of my presence
after he had already touched me
The cellular makeup of my actual body after

■

I don't know if it was a waste to forgive

It was a waste to forgive
forgiving is hard
unrewarding work

It is a waste to sing slang
just to charm

It is a waste to participate in a myth
that never dies

Pitless affection is a waste
sole pitlessness is a waste

It was a waste cutting my nails
so I could text him

It was a waste for my friend to have a vasectomy

■

I am sometimes around kids

It infects me

It makes me listen to Kendrick Lamar
in order to regain myself

Then I drown and wake up and do it again

I don't blame the children tho
I don't want to play with them tho
I don't want to not want them tho
I don't want to not want to watch them tho
I don't want to want to not want to want them tho

■

It is a waste
to go to Coney Island
if you are trying to forget the past, of all things

It's a waste cause actually it can feel great
to not be able to see and then to get to forget
some of the past!

Your own past, that is,
whilst being tossed around
on the toys of grandparents

I got really exhilarated
being touched and after
watching the black water
toss nothing alive

In our scorching shelter,
we could do anything, we realized,
so we loved each other
till we fought and each
of us said that was not
our style but you have to
stop kidding yourself
at some point and why not
do it on the beach

If I could tell him now I
would tell him: why not
do it on the beach
and make up quietly

Then you can go home

■

The narcissist
expertly wastes
his lover

Her soul is wasted
by just being around him

He makes the most
profound waste
of the soul;

His life utterly
depends on it

■

My love's memory lives on
in the other physical love
of others

■

I pay my friends to teach me
I pray I am taught
My friends are broke
We've overpaid our enemies
My friends have hearts
We're broke at
our own feast

■

I'm on a plane again
There is zero sense of movement and it's absurd
and it's violent to fly and everyone's asleep

Clouds are hard to believe
but not unbelievable

Torque get less real
as it is ably demonstrated

Feeling torque is a unique feeling

The pilot has come out of the pit
He is having some sort of beverage
I hope he is terribly, terribly drunk
I am the worst person on the plane

■

I have driven three of the same car
I love

I have replaced its parts so slowly
it has not stayed the same car

I have falsely asserted a consistent
spirit to my car, which I nourish

I have totaled a car I have tried
to impress people in

I have totally
impressed them in it

Once I learned about cruise control
it became hard to stop

Once I drove 34 miles on cruise control
That's my record

Once I became weak
for the rest of my life

I never talked my way out of a ticket
Once I didn't drive to him
when I totally could have

All my speeding tickets
were worth it and
I would do them again

Once I got a ticket for driving
without a seatbelt because I was
driving great without a seatbelt
and I was really happy
until I was finally convicted

The charge is called:
"Unrestrained driver (no seatbelt)"
and that money which I paid
to the state for wanting to drive
in this vulnerable state
has funded something and I hope
it is working out for that something
and that something good has come
out of my driving in this unrestrained manner
in my highly spirited automobile
towards no one

Index of first lines

Emily Toder is the author of the collections *Beachy Head* and *Science*, both from Coconut Books, and the chapbooks *It's Not Over Yet* (If a Leaf Falls Press), *Brushes With* (Tarpaulin Sky Press), *No Land* (Brave Men Press), and *I Hear a Boat* (Duets Books). She lives in New York.

39897874R00064

Made in the USA
Middletown, DE
24 March 2019